CONTENTS

ISBN 0-87666-822-8

Photography
G. Axelrod: 88, 89. Dr. H. R. Axelrod: 14. T. Brosset: 19. G. Ebben: 31. H. V. Lacey: title page, 12, 32. C. Naether: 46 (top). Courtesy of San Diego Zoo: 10, 11, 15, 18, 22, 23. V. Serbin: endpapers, 7, 16, 17, 26, 27, 30, 34, 35, 36, 37, 46 (bottom), 47, 48, 49, 50, 51, 54, 55, 62, 63, 66, 67, 70, 71, 72, 73, 74-75, 76, 78, 79, 80 (top), 81, 82, 83, 86, 87, 90, 91. L. Van der Meid: 33, 77. Courtesy of Vogelpark Walsrode: 6, 80 (bottom).

Distributed in the U.S. by T.F.H. Publications, Inc., 211 West Sylvania Avenue, PO Box 427, Neptune, NJ 07753; in England by T.F.H. (Gt. Britain) Ltd., 13 Nutley Lane, Reigate, Surrey; in Canada to the pet trade by Rolf C. Hagen Ltd., 3225 Sartelon Street, Montreal 382, Quebec; in Canada to the book trade by H & L Pet Supplies, Inc., 27 Kingston Crescent, Kitchener, Ontario N28 2T6; in Southeast Asia by Y.W. Ong, 9 Lorong 36 Geylang, Singapore 14; in Australia and the South Pacific by Pet Imports Pty. Ltd., P.O. Box 149, Brookvale 2100, N.S.W. Australia; in South Africa by Valid Agencies, P.O. Box 51901, Randburg 2125 South Africa. Published by T.F.H. Publications, Inc., Ltd., the British Crown Colony of Hong Kong.

TAMING AND TRAINING RINGNECK PARAKEETS

RISA TEITLER
PROFESSIONAL TRAINER

Left: Ringnecked parakeets derive their popular name from the "ring" around the neck as evident in this blue mutation of *Psittacula krameri. Below:* A young ringnecked parakeet and a budgerigar will sit side by side on a bird stand if trained properly and acquainted with one another at an early age.

Introduction

Ringnecked parakeets take their name from the best known species of the genus *(Psittacula)*, the Rose-ringed Parakeet. Extremely common in its range, the two subspecies of the Rose-ringed are called Indian and African Ringnecks. In all the ringnecks a patch of black beneath the beak extends backwards to form at least a "moustache," or further, making a ring around the neck. Even in the moustached species, the contrasting head and neck colors complete the effect of a ring.

Ringnecks are not at all similar to budgies, which many people call "parakeets." They are much larger than budgies; one of the species of ringnecks attains a total length of twenty-three inches. Most are between twelve and sixteen inches from the top of the head to the tip of the tail. The tail is long, especially the two central tail feathers, which may have rounded tips. You will also find these birds referred to as "long-tailed parakeets."

The beak is large and well adapted to eating fruit and corn. Ringnecks are also voracious chewers of wood and bark. The wings are tapered and long, for strong, swift flight. The birds often congregate in family groups or small to large flocks. While in flight, they call to one another. The call is often accompanied by dilation of the pupils. Pupillary dilation is an interesting behavior that also occurs during courtship or when one bird is making aggressive movements toward a rival. Eye color is a brilliant red, gold, yellow, or white, with a dark inner ring on the iris.

Compared to many of their parrot relatives, ringnecks exhibit more obvious plumage differences between the sexes. One drawback for the prospective breeder is the fact that male plumage is attained no earlier than eighteen months of age and may take two full molts (two years) to appear. For this reason many breeders have mistakenly bought young male birds as females. There seem to be far more male ringnecks than females.

All ringnecks have a body color that is basically green, but they are marked with hues of blue, rose, yellow, white, and black. One species has a brilliant purple breast. Color variations of the normal plumage have appeared, notably lutino and blue. These mutations are beautiful and can be bred consistently in controlled breeding environments.

The natural range of ringnecks is wide, extending from west central Africa through India to Borneo. The best known ringneck, the Rose-ringed Parakeet, *Psittacula krameri*, has the widest distribution of any parrot. Of the perhaps fifteen psittaculid species (and many more subspecies), only a few are frequently obtainable.

HEALTH AND LONGEVITY

Ringnecked parakeets are very hardy birds that adapt well to cold weather, when acclimated properly. In many climates, ringnecks can live outdoors the year around, provided that the diet and shelter are adequate. Illness is rarely seen in well-maintained pet birds. When it does occur, it is usually due to stress from an overcrowded or dirty environment or from poor nutrition.

The most frequent medical problem that I have seen in ringnecks is injury. In large colonies that are kept in flight cages injuries are bound to occur because ringnecks have a very strong pecking order. Male birds are constantly competing for status with each other. When the birds are in breeding condition, the flock should be watched carefully to prevent serious injury to any member of the group. The birds will gang up on a single bird if it seems to be easily pecked by others in the group. If you detect a situation where one bird is being chased a great deal, you should remove it to another cage.

The life span of ringnecks is close to twenty years. Environment and genetic background are determining factors in the life span of any individual ringneck. Some may live just eleven years and seem old, while others may reach nineteen years and appear youthful.

Reproductive maturity is attained at approximately two years. Although some birds may breed at an earlier age, most wait two years or more before beginning to nest successfully. Once mature, a healthy ringneck will continue to breed for most of its adult life.

PERSONALITY

In ringnecked parakeets personality varies considerably from bird to bird. There are a few general comments that

1 Whether in flight (1) or repose (2), *Psittacula krameri* is a beautiful bird. The individual shown is of the lutino color variety.

can be made, however. The wild ringneck is a flighty, high-strung bird. It constantly flies from one side of the cage to the other or jumps away from you when you approach.

The ringneck is a fine pet bird when tamed. Taming them is not as easily accomplished as it is with Cockatiels. In this respect ringnecks are more like conures. They are somewhat resistant at first. They do not want to give up their independence—and they are very independent. With well-planned, dedicated training your ringneck will become an outgoing, friendly bird. The acrobatic comic will show through once the bird learns to trust you.

Curiosity is another trait of ringnecked parakeets. They have excellent speech potential and will learn to talk if trained. The voice is fairly high pitched, but it is much clearer than that of a budgie.

Ringnecks are meticulous about their plumage and love to bathe. Being very active birds and strong fliers, they require a large cage.

Some of the Plum-heads that I have owned chewed holes in the plaster, so guard against damage to woodwork, picture frames and houseplants.

Be aware of their aggressiveness toward newcomers before placing a new bird (after quarantine, of course) in the same cage with an established resident. Ringnecks may become jealous of other birds sharing your attention.

Ringnecks (shown opposite is a Moustached Parakeet, *Psittacula alexandri*) at rest are sedate and have an almost regal appearance—but they can suddenly change into delightful clowns.

1. Slaty-headed Parakeet, *Psittacula himalayana*. 2. Moustached Parakeet, *Psittacula alexandri*.

2→

Left: Ringnecks love to perch high up in their cages. A swing or a brass key ring hanging from the cage top will quickly become your bird's favorite spot. *Below:* The superb health of this young Plum-head is indicated by its clear, bright eyes, clean nostrils and alert expression.

How To Buy a Ringnecked Parakeet

CHOOSING A SOURCE

There are two main sources for ringnecked parakeets in the United States and abroad. The easiest to locate is a reliable bird shop with a *good* reputation. The second is far more difficult to find: the independent breeder. If you know someone who has a ringneck, find out where he got it. Look around for both a good pet shop and a good breeder before committing yourself to a purchase.

Pet shops with good reputations usually have a clientele of local residents. But no matter how highly a friend praises a particular shop or how badly he pans it, take the time to visit all the possible sources and form your own opinion.

2

←1

1. Male Rose-ringed Parakeet, *Psittacula krameri*. 2. Close-up of the beautiful Nepalese Alexandrine Parakeet, *Psittacula eupatria nipalensis*.

You may live in an area where the ringnecked parakeet is not a commonly stocked item. In some parts of the country they are rarely found, unless the shop owner special-orders them. If you can find a shop that has connections with a breeder of ringnecks, go ahead and have them special-order a youngster for you. Even if you have to wait until a bird is hatched and old enough to leave the parents, it is worth the wait.

Choose with care the source that you buy from. Don't rush into the purchase of your first ringneck just because one is available on the premises. Look around the shop and pay attention to the types of accessories that are kept in stock. Bird cages of different sizes and in various price ranges is one priority. Use your eyes to check up on the cleanliness of the shop, especially the bottoms of the bird cages and the food and water dishes. Make a note of the seed and supplements that are present in the cages of the birds on display. Is the seed fresh? Does the water look dirty? Does it have a supplement? Is there any evidence of fresh fruits or vegetables in the cage?

Ringnecks should be fed both parakeet mix and sunflower seed. Fruits and vegetables should also be given daily. So check to see if the birds are being fed properly in the pet shop. A well-fed bird in a clean cage is a good recommendation for the shop.

The best pet shops will offer a wide selection of supplements. These include such items as water-soluble vitamins and powdered vitamin and mineral supplements and oils. A supply of reading material on the type of bird that you have in mind is also noteworthy.

The shop may sell prepared seed mixtures for the various types of birds that it carries. Taste the seed to see if it is fresh. Smell it and look at it. Usually, you will find the pet shop your best source of bird seed and supplements. Do not buy bird seed at your supermarket, unless you run out and can't get to the shop. Supermarket bird seed is often old, having sat in cartons and on a shelf for months. There is not enough consumer demand for bird seed at the supermarket.

If your pet shop does not sell seed, try to find a farm supply store (in some localities a farm supply store can't be found; in other areas it is one of the main shops in town.)

WHAT SPECIES SHOULD YOU BUY?

The most commonly available of all ringnecks, as mentioned earlier, is the Rose-ringed Parakeet, *Psittacula krameri*. Males have a beautiful rose-colored ring in addition to the black one around the neck. It is by far the least expensive of all ringnecked parakeets, being the most common. It makes a fine pet and a good talker if properly trained.

If your pet shop has six or more Rose-ringed Parakeets and none of them has adult male plumage, the chances are that you are looking at a group of very young birds. Since the great majority of ringnecks are males, do not shy away from buying a bird in this group. It may in fact be the best possible purchase!

The Plum-headed Parakeet, *Psittacula cyanocephala*, is more colorful than the Rose-ring, less common and usually a bit more expensive. Again a group of birds that all look like females (lacking the black ring and bright purple head) is probably a group of youngsters. Plum-headed parakeets are imported from Malaysia, and some are bred here in the United States for the pet trade. The Plum-head is just as good a talker as the Rose-ring; if you can spend a little more money, go ahead and buy the Plum-head.

The Alexandrine Parakeet, *Psittacula eupatria*, is very similar to the Rose-ring in coloration. The most noticeable difference is in the size of the bird. Alexandrines are quite large. They are much more expensive than either the Plum-head or the Rose-ring. Most Alexandrines are kept as aviary birds by hopeful breeders.

21

1. Blue mutation of *Psittacula krameri*. 2. Plum-headed Parakeet, *Psittacula cyanocephala*.

2

← 1

The beautiful Moustached Parakeet, *Psittacula alexandri,* is inexpensive and one of the more popular of the ringnecks. Like the Rose-ring and Plum-head, it is both imported and bred in the U.S.A.

The four above-mentioned birds are the most readily acquired of the ringnecked parakeets. All make good talkers when trained. The other species of ringnecks may appear occasionally at your local shop, but it is unlikely.

In addition to the normal ringnecks, you may come across lutino or blue mutations. These color variations are at least two to three times as costly as the wild-colored individuals. They are gorgeous birds and make just as fine pets as the normals. Their potential for speech and long life is also equal to that of normal birds.

IDENTIFYING A HEALTHY RINGNECK

The most important factor in your success with a new ringneck is your ability to choose a healthy bird. Whether you want a pet or a breeder, the same basic criteria apply. When you find yourself ready to buy, you will very likely have to choose a bird from a group in a cage. Do not have one of the pet-shop employees choose a bird for you. His job is to sell you a bird. Your job is to choose the right one.

Healthy birds are both physically and mentally well. How can you determine a bird's mental health? Watch the behavior of all the birds in the cage. Those that stand off by themselves, remain on the cage bottom or run from the other birds may have emotional problems. Use your common sense when bird watching. Stand back from the cage, out of sight if possible, to avoid inhibiting the birds' natural interaction.

Be aware that female birds are often less aggressive than male birds, so if you are looking for a pair and there is no obviously mature female present, watch for a more reticent individual. Make sure that the reticent bird fulfills all of the qualifications for a healthy bird.

We have established that a healthy bird interacts freely with others in its peer group. After you have observed the birds for a while and have picked out one or two good-looking candidates for purchase, identify them to a pet shop employee by noting some physical characteristic. Now get ready to give your choices a thorough examination. Ask the seller to hold the bird while you look it over. Know what you want to look at and be as quick as you can. Holding a bird for extended periods of time subjects it to enormous stress and should be avoided.

Check the bird's *respiration*. This is best done when the ringneck is sitting quietly on a perch. Watch the breast. Normal breathing is slow and regular. There is no noticeable sound when a healthy bird breathes. If you can hear the bird's respiration, the bird may be asthmatic or have some other undesirable condition of the lungs.

When a bird is being held for physical examination its respiration is going to be speeded up and heavier than normal. Remember to notice the bird's respiration before removing it from the flight cage.

Next, check the bird's *vent*. If there is soiling on the feathers surrounding the vent, disqualify the bird. No further examination is necessary, for you should never purchase a bird with a soiled vent.

Look carefully at the bird's *eyes*. The surface of the eye itself must be clear and bright. The pupils must respond to light. If there is any cloudiness on the surface of the eye, the bird may have eye trouble in the form of a cataract. Eyes that look swollen, teary or dull may indicate illness.

The *feet* and *legs* are next on the list. There should be no sores or calluses on either the legs or feet. Birds with missing toes or lumps on the legs or feet should be rejected. One missing toe is not too serious a disability, especially if you do not plan to breed the bird. However, even one missing toe should reduce the cost of the bird. If the seller does not agree, don't buy the bird. Lumps or thick spots on the leg

1. Be certain that your ringnecked parakeet's wing is properly clip-ped before taking the bird outside. If the bird flies out of your house and perches on a fence or a tree, approach slowly and do not frighten it. 2. Millet spray is a favorite food of ringnecks and can be used to reward the bird for good behavior.

may be old, healed fractures. Again, if this does not reduce the selling price, look for another bird.

Be certain to check the *feces* of the bird. Of course this is difficult to do if the bird was housed in a cage with many other ringnecks. Look carefully at the bottom of the cage. If the droppings look normal, don't worry about the bird in your hand. But, if the cage bottom is full of bad-looking evacuations, reject the bird.

Normal droppings are dark green and white when dry. They have solid form and are not watery or runny. Avoid birds with watery, all white, all green, or off-color stools. The droppings should not be light green, brown, yellow, orange or black and tarry. When you are restraining the bird during the examination, it may pass a dropping. Very often, nervousness will cause the bird to have a watery stool. If all of the droppings in the cage look all right, don't worry. Just make sure that the bird passes all of the other tests for health.

The nasal openings are called the *nares*. Both nares must be dirt-free. There should be no scratches or cuts on them. Red spots and scabs on the fleshy areas around the nares are undesirable. Birds with noticeable discharge from the nares should never be purchased. Sometimes, the nares may seem to be clear of debris, but the upper part of the beak will have some indications of nasal discharge. In this case, do not buy the bird, for it may have a condition that flares up at night or in the morning, such as sinus trouble.

Feel the bird's *breast* to be certain that it has "good weight." Good weight means that there is plenty of flesh on either side of the breastbone. If the breastbone protrudes and you can grasp it between your thumb and forefinger, the bird is thin. Of course there are varying degrees of thinness; but if you have any doubt about the bird, don't buy it. Thin birds may have any number of medical problems, the *least* of which is probably serious. Thin birds may have worm infestation, or they may not be eating due to illness.

Never, never buy a thin bird, even if the seller drops the price.

The last important criterion for good health is adequate *plumage*. Young birds have duller plumage than their older counterparts but should not have any bare patches of skin showing through the feathers. Do not mistake a bird with scanty feathering for a baby. Once a baby bird leaves the nest, it should have feathers covering the entire body. Sometimes ringnecks pluck out a few feathers during molting, but this should never be extensive enough to show skin underneath.

The larger feathers of the wings and tail should not be excessively broken. Of course you should expect some breakage to have occurred during shipping and quarantine, but use your common sense. Birds with many broken feathers on the wings and tail may be feather chewers or may have been pecked by other birds. It takes quite a long time for many broken feathers to molt out and new ones to grow.

WHAT A SICK BIRD LOOKS LIKE

A sick ringneck tries to hide its affliction, for it does not want to appear weak. The classic signs of illness do not become obvious until a bird is *really* sick. The following describes a sick ringneck.

The bird sits off by itself in the presence of others of its own kind, not interacting with the group. Both feet remain on the perch, yet the bird seems to be resting. (Only one foot should remain on the perch when a healthy bird is resting.) The eyes may be closed or partially closed. The feathers may be ruffled up to conserve body heat, or they may be matted down, the wings held out from the body slightly to rid the bird of excess heat.

Discharge may be apparent around the eyes or the nostrils. There may be a clog in one or both nares, or the beak may be stained with discharge from the nares. The

1. Use your free hand and your voice to distract the bird from jumping off your hand. 2. A pair of Derbyan Parakeets, *Psittacula derbiana*. The male is the bird with the red bill.

feathers surrounding the vent may be stained. The underside of the tail may be soiled.

Feces on the cage bottom beneath the bird will look loose and have bad form or no form at all. Wrong-color stools are obvious on the cage bottom.

The bird may or may not appear thin (its feathers could be too ruffled up to tell). Respiration will be too heavy, irregular or labored. A rasping sound may accompany respiration.

Sick birds have lolling heads and are, overall, listless and indifferent to what goes on around them. Often, a sick bird is very easy to grab hold of and does not even attempt to bite.

These are the classic symptoms of illness. They do not usually appear until the bird is very, very ill, possibly at death's door. However, be aware that not all sick birds look sick. They try to hide it for as long as they can.

2

Ringnecked parakeets of all types (1. Rosering Parakeets, *Psittacula krameri;* 2. male Moustached Parakeet, *Psittacula alexandri)* in good health carry themselves proudly and show an active interest in their surroundings. Sick birds, however, look droopy and show no vitality.

Left: A handful of sunflower seeds on your open palm is a good way to make friends with a new ringnecked parakeet. *Below:* Use a vitamin-mineral powder on the bird's fruit and vegetables every day. Sprinkle it on lightly and use it in addition to a water soluble vitamin.

Care and Feeding

When you bring your new bird home, place it on a standard maintenance diet. The daily diet should include high-quality sunflower seed, fresh parakeet mix, one or two raw peanuts (not roasted), fresh water with a vitamin supplement, and fresh fruits and vegetables.

The vitamin supplement that you use in the water may be obtained at the pet shop. There are a number of good products manufactured especially for birds. Look these over and choose one that can simply be added to the bird's drinking water. You may also want to buy a powdered vitamin-mineral supplement to sprinkle on the fresh fruit that your bird gets.

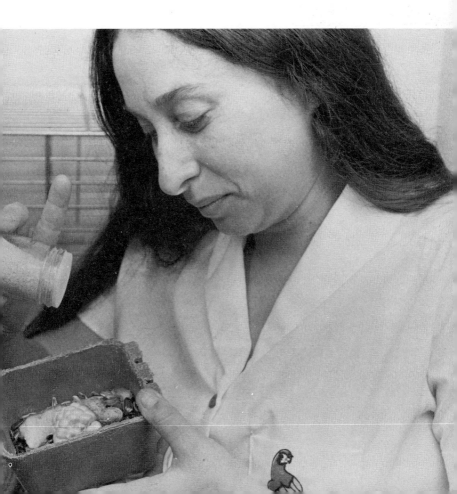

2

1. Cups that can be removed from outside the cage are very useful, because they make the job of filling the cups easier. Additionally, they allow the cup-filling operation to be performed without unduly disturbing the occupants of the cage. The cups should be refilled with fresh, high-quality seed on a daily basis. 2. This ringnecked parakeet is hanging from a swing in its cage to grab a few bites of millet spray. 3. Millet sprays are excellent treats for ringnecked parakeets and many other parrots as well. A fresh spray can be twisted through the bars of the cage every two or three days as a treat. Don't, however, make the mistake of feeding too many treats; ringnecked parakeets need a balanced diet.

3

Feed the bird two or three different fruits and vegetables each day. Examples are apple (ringnecks love apple, but don't feed it exclusively), citrus fruits, banana, mango, melon, corn on the cob, green beans, peas, squash, celery and any other fruits and vegetables in season. Always feed fruits and vegetables raw; cooking removes much of the nutritional value.

In addition to fruits and vegetables, feed your ringneck a portion of a fresh green leafy vegetable each day. Use romaine lettuce, chickory or endive. Iceberg lettuce has little food value, so don't bother to feed it.

You may also include a dish of fresh gravel (grit) with oyster shell. Some of the better gravel mixtures contain charcoal, but never try to add charcoal yourself, for you should not use briquette charcoal. In addition to the gravel, be certain to include a cuttlebone or mineral block. These mineral supplements are very important and must be included in the diet of all ringnecks.

Treats that you may want to offer include millet spray, fresh branches with the leaves, and egg biscuits. Do not feed hard-boiled egg, as it may get lost in the cage, spoil, and poison the bird. Use the egg biscuit that you can get from your pet shop. Soaked wheat bread is loved by some ringnecks and hated by others. The seed bells that you can find at the pet store are fine, but your bird may pay no attention to them.

It is important to be certain that the seed you feed your bird is the freshest possible. For this reason, buy your seed from the feed store or pet shop, not the grocery.

Use separate dishes for sunflower seed and parakeet mix. This makes it easier to see how much of each item the bird eats. It also saves on waste when you blow off the chaff. Place the small pieces of fruit and vegetables on top of the seeds, along with the raw peanuts. The leafy vegetables may be hung along with millet spray on the wire inside the cage.

Washing the food and water dishes is the best single way to ensure your pet ringneck's good health. Every day, wash the water dish with soap and water; rinse it well. Refill with water and vitamins. You may have to wash the seed dishes every day if you have a messy bird. Most of the ringnecks I own are neat, so the seed dishes have to be washed only every two or three days. Dry the seed dishes completely before refilling with seed. Damp dishes make moldy seed.

The cage bottom must be cleaned daily. You may cover the cage bottom with newspaper, kitty litter or gravel paper. I don't use gravel paper because gravel is to eat, not walk on. Don't use sand; it is too messy and may bring in parasite eggs.

Besides cleaning the cage bottom daily, be sure to wash it thoroughly at least once a week, more often if you can. Dry it completely before replacing it in the cage. The best cages for ringnecks come with wire grills that sit above the cage bottom. The grill will become soiled with droppings and must be kept clean. Wash it at the same time you wash the bottom tray.

The cage itself should not require washing very often, unless your bird gets it dirty. Use mild soap and water to wash cage bars.

The perches should be cleaned periodically to remove any food debris or fecal matter. Buy a perch scraper or use sandpaper for this purpose. Perches may be washed and dried thoroughly; it is better not to have the bird stand on wet perches.

BATHING THE BIRD

Most ringnecks enjoy their bath and need very little coaxing to jump in and splash around. You can buy a commercial bird bath, but usually they are too small for the average ringneck. Try giving the bird a sturdy dish with tepid water. Place it on the cage bottom, sit back and watch the show. Birds taking a bath are so funny to watch. They splash the water with their wings, jump in with both feet and dunk their heads under water. When they are finished bathing they look half drowned and completely happy. For hours they will sit and preen their clean feathers until every feather is back in place and shining.

Your bird may not take to bathing in a dish at first; give it time. If it absolutely refuses to bathe in a dish, try using a spray bottle filled with tepid water to mist the bird. Commercial bird sprays may be used, but water will do just as well.

The bath should be allowed only in the morning or early afternoon on warm, sunny days. Bathing late in the day can bring on illness, because the bird may not dry enough before dusk.

SPRAYING FOR PARASITES

It is unlikely that a well-cared-for ringnecked parakeet will have problems with parasites. When you first buy it, however, your bird may have a few. The most common—lice and mites—infest the heavy feathers of the wing and tail. Both are fairly easy to eradicate.

Use a commercially prepared bird spray. Follow the directions on the can. Most of these preparations will advise removing all bird food before spraying the bird and the cage. Be sure that you do. Do not drench the bird with insecticide even if it is made for birds. A new bird should not be made wet, or it may become ill. Do not spray more often than is recommended on the container. As directed, spray both the cage and bird.

Birds that reside in outdoor aviaries will probably have a few parasites in their feathers. This is nothing to be too concerned about as long as you keep the infestation under control. The only way to accomplish this is to periodically spray the aviary floor, perches and fittings. Outdoor aviaries need far more maintenance to keep them free of parasites than do indoor cages.

CAGES AND ACCESSORIES

You must have an adequate cage before bringing the bird home. Of course you may buy the bird and the cage at the same time, but it is better to have the cage already set up and in a good location before transporting the bird from the pet shop.

Ringnecks are very active and therefore need a good-sized cage. A large budgie cage will not do. The smallest acceptable dimensions are 20 inches square and 30 inches high. Anything smaller will cramp the bird.

The wires should be spaced at about ¾ to 1 inch apart, to provide the right grip for the birds' feet. Ringnecks have fairly large feet. The wire should be of a fairly heavy gauge and unpainted. Nickel plating results in a silver-colored finish and is excellent for parrot cages. It resists rust and wear for many years if properly maintained. You may prefer a gold-colored finish, which is fine too, but it seems to tarnish more easily than the nickel plate.

The perches should be made of wood with a diameter of no less than ¾ inches. Remember the ringneck's big feet. Perches of a smaller diameter will cramp the toes. Natural wood perches are preferred to dowels, because they provide the advantage of various grip sizes. This helps exercise the feet.

Parrot cages come with at least two food dishes; some have four. The dishes are usually made of plastic. Glass is nice because it is easy to clean, but it does break when dropped. The same can be said for ceramic-coated dishes. Metal dishes are fine for seed but undesirable for water, unless they are aluminum. Metal dishes always tarnish and some become pitted with use. If the cage you buy has only two dishes, get a couple of extras. Budgie-sized dishes are too small; get parrot dishes.

If your cage doesn't have a swing, buy one. Ringnecks love high places and usually spend their nights sleeping on the swing.

A cage cover is not usually necessary, but in very cold climates you will want to cover the cage at night. Be sure that there are no loose threads hanging from the cover, because the bird could get tangled up. Ringnecks love to chew, so don't invest a lot of money in a cage cover. The one that you embroider especially for the bird cage won't be beautiful for long, so don't get too upset when you find holes in it. Covers are handy when the bird has had a bath. Cover the cage back, top and sides. Leave the front open.

A bird stand is a valuable piece of equipment, especially if you plan to tame the ringneck. Make your T-stand or buy one ready-made. Some are very attractive, but costly. The best bird stands are sturdy floor models, about 4 to 4½ feet tall. They may have food cups that attach to the perch. Some have a tray to catch debris. Look at the commercially made stands at your pet shop. You may decide to build one based on the designs you see, or you might just go ahead and buy one.

The crossbar that your bird stands on should have the same diameter as the perches in the cage (¾ to 1 inch). A little bit larger is also fine. The crossbar should be made of wood, not plastic or metal. The vertical piece can be made of almost any strong material. Attaching the crossbar to the vertical should be studied carefully if you are making your own stand. Be certain that the crossbar is secure. At the same time you may want to make provision for changing the crossbar after a while and replacing it with a new one. Stands are great if your bird spends time out of the cage or goes visiting with you. Like anything else, you must teach the ringneck to sit on the stand and remain there.

Toys should be examined carefully before being given to the bird. Bells are fine toys, if the clappers are secure inside. Wooden ladders and chewy toys can be found at the pet shop. Some enterprising companies are now marketing a complete line of toys for parrots. These should be available through your pet dealer. A chain dog collar hanging from the cage roof can become the bird's favorite toy. Just make sure that it is heavy enough to prevent the bird from twisting it around its body. You may want to buy the bird a mirror, but most birds are very hard to speech-train when given a mirror. So if you want to teach the bird to talk, don't put mirrors in the cage. The pet shop may have one or two bird playgrounds. These are fine and in many cases can take the place of the bird stand. Most birds become very attached to their playground and do not want to leave it to go back to the cage.

OTHER EQUIPMENT

If you plan to attempt taming, you will need training sticks. Two dowels, one long and one short, are the minimum needed. The long dowel should be 24 to 30 inches long, the short dowel 16 to 18 inches. Both should have a diameter of 1 to 1½ inches. Natural wood training sticks are fine.

Carriers are very handy and can be made of wood, heavy cardboard or molded plastic. You will need a carrier to take the bird on car rides (if you plan to) or to the vet, if the need arises. The box that the pet shop gives you to bring the bird home in will not last forever.

Bird nets are not really necessary with a single family pet. In an aviary situation they are indispensable. Nets come with both long and short handles. Get one of each if you are planning an outdoor aviary.

Gloves are not recommended for any reason. Some people feel that gloves must be worn during the taming of a bird. This is a foolish attitude. If you work carefully, you probably won't get bitten too often. Birds are frightened of gloves, for most have been grabbed several times by people wearing gloves before ever getting to the pet shop. If you must have gloves, buy a tight-fitting pair in a neutral shade. Golf gloves are fine.

TRANSPORTING YOUR BIRD HOME

Transport your bird in a box, not the cage. There are several reasons for using a box, provided it has ventilation. First, the bird will remain calmer if its vision is restricted. In an open cage the sights and sounds of rushing traffic will make a bird frantic. A closed box also provides protection from sudden changes in temperature. Obviously, an open cage cannot protect the bird in this way. A frightened bird may catch its wings between the cage wire, but that cannot happen in a box. Box carriers are especially important in the winter when moving from a heated store to the cold outdoors and back to a heated house.

Although a box affords some protection from rainfall, it is not recommended that you transport a newly acquired ringneck in the rain. Have the store hold the bird for you until the weather clears. Better yet, wait for the rain to stop, and then go home.

If possible, transport the bird during daylight hours. Once in its new environment, the ringneck will have the opportunity to observe the coming of dusk before settling down for the night.

ACCLIMATING NEW BIRDS

Whether you buy one bird or a dozen, you must acclimate the new arrival carefully. This is done by having all of the suggested foods and vitamin-mineral supplements on hand by the time you bring the bird home.

Feed your new ringnecked parakeet in the morning and give it plenty of free time. In other words, even if you are anxious to begin taming the bird, give it a few days of adjustment time before putting it through the rigors of training.

Do not keep your new bird up late at night. Allow it to go to roost when the sun goes down, as it would naturally. Keep the bird cage out of drafts and away from doors and windows. Cover the new bird at night.

Restrict the amount of time you spend looking at the bird. Most new ringnecks will fly to the upper back wall of the cage when you approach. This is hardly restful for a new bird.

Every morning look carefully at the droppings from the night before. If they look normal, fine. If they are abnormal on the first day, don't worry. If, however, they are still abnormal (according to the criterion of good health) on the second and third days, take a sample to a vet for examination.

You will be taking a stool sample to a vet after five to seven days for a worm check regardless of how the droppings appear. Internal parasites are not unusual in newly imported birds. Don't be alarmed; most are easy to eradicate. But be absolutely certain to obtain your veterinarian's help in diagnosing and treating internal parasites.

Birds that will be living in outdoor facilities should first be acclimated indoors to allow time to feather in completely and to give you a chance to check on their food intake and droppings. Do not move new birds outdoors in the fall or winter. Spring and summer are the best times of year for introducing new birds to the outdoor aviary.

Keep track of the bird's intake of food, both seeds and soft foods (fruits and vegetables). Many birds do not eat at all on the first day in a new environment. If your new bird has not eaten for two or three days, you should take action. Notify the pet shop where you bought the bird and inquire what the previous diet was. You may also want to consult a vet and perhaps begin feeding an appetite stimulant.

To improve a bird's appetite try feeding each item of the diet in a separate cup. You can put the peanuts on top of the sunflower seeds but put only one or two in at a time. Don't cover up the seed with either peanuts or fruit. Put the soft foods in a separate cup. Some birds will refuse fruits and vegetables at first. The most important thing for

1. Ringnecks maintained in roomy aviaries generally have more opportunity to exercise than caged birds. 2. These two young ringnecks are sitting on their swings and waiting to be fed. Note the heavy gauge of wire used to construct the cage. Ringnecks are powerful chewers and must be housed in spacious cages with strong wire. 3. A water-soluble vitamin made especially for birds is essential. Wash and refill the water cup daily.

a new bird to eat is seed. Seed keeps its weight up and the droppings normal. Too much fruit and too little seed can cause diarrhea.

The appetite stimulants your vet can supply can be in liquid or paste form. Try to get something to put in the water rather than something that must be put down the bird's throat.

Always be certain that the new bird is eating well before placing it in the outdoor aviary or beginning to tame it. Do not give the bird a bath during the acclimation period.

In review, the acclimation period is the time to get your new ringnecked parakeet on the right diet. This is when you will take stool samples to the vet for worm checks and, if necessary, treat the bird for worms. You will make a daily check on droppings to catch any possible illnesses in advance of serious complications. During acclimation you will also get to know and respect your bird. You will hear it make its first sounds and see it play for the first time in its new home. You will also discover that birds sleep during the day as well as during the night.

3

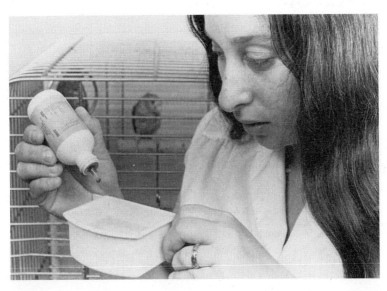

Left: Offer your ringneck a piece of fruit or a peanut once you have it perching quietly on a bird stand. This will encourage the bird to remain sitting on the stand. *Below:* Never strike or drop a ringneck if it bites you during a lesson. If necessary, work with a training stick for many lessons before offering your hand.

Training the Ringneck Parakeet

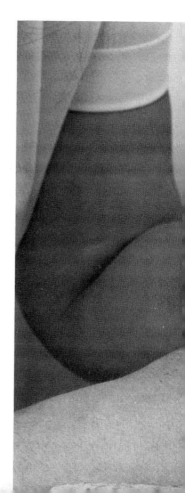

To begin taming your ringnecked parakeet you will have to first decide on a suitable training area, and you should clip one of the bird's wings. You must also make a firm commitment to follow through on any training that you begin.

QUALITIES OF A GOOD TRAINER

Only one person should handle the bird during the first taming lessons. This person can be either male or female. He or she must have a calm disposition and plenty of time to devote to taming. Nervous trainers have a difficult time dealing with wild birds.

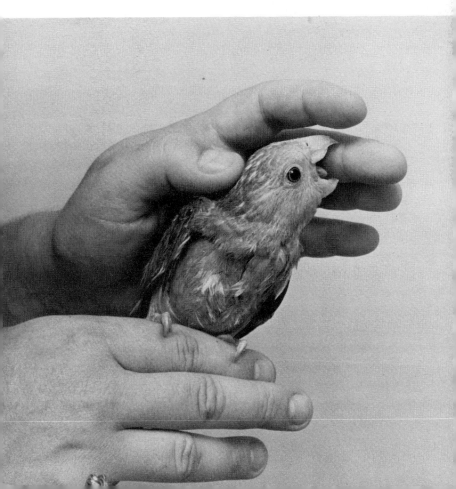

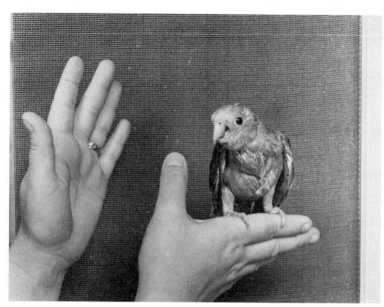

1. Use an open palm at the bird's eye level to focus its attention on your face instead of your hand when you begin hand taming. 2. A very young ringneck might allow you to touch its back lightly, but never force petting on your bird.

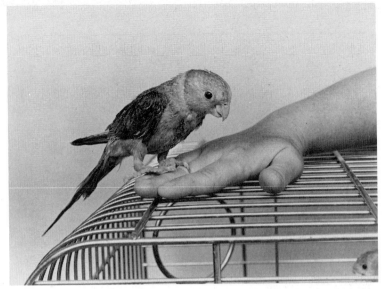

3

3. When you open the cage door, the ringneck will usually climb to the top. Offer your hand for the bird to perch on after it is stick-trained. 4. Talk to the bird to attract its attention as you slide a flat hand, fingers together, under the bird's feet.

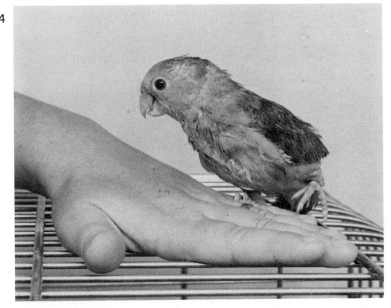

4

The best trainer for a wild bird is someone who has respect for the creature and does not feel compelled to strike the bird if it should bite. Young children should not attempt to tame any parrot, not even a small bird like a ringneck. Children do not understand that birds bite out of fear, and they may think that the wild bird dislikes them personally. It is also a bad idea to let a child be exposed to the possibility of getting bitten; ringnecks can inflict a painful wound.

A good trainer is able to formulate a sensible training program and stick with it.

THE TRAINING AREA

It is best to prepare an area for taming somewhere besides the family room. A small, uncluttered room works well. Try using the bathroom or an extra bedroom—a place where you can close the door and be alone with the new bird. You may use a hallway, but you will have to barricade the ends. Rooms with lots of furniture and curtains are very hard to work in because you will be constantly chasing the bird out from under something or trying to retrieve it from the curtain rod.

If the floor is not carpeted, you should be sure to pad the floor adequately to prevent injury to the bird. Untamed birds always take a few falls during the first lessons. A sheet is not adequate padding for a stone or tile floor. Cover any mirrors and windows. Some birds will make a mad dash for the outside if they think they can reach it.

The taming area should have a quiet atmosphere, free from television noise or the conversation of other family members. Soft background music may be used to your advantage, for it often calms a nervous bird.

Work alone with the bird until you have it fairly tame. Then ask someone else in to try working with it. The first lessons are frightening for the new bird, so only one person should be in the taming area with it.

You will have to bring the T-stand into the taming area and probably the cage also. Have your two training sticks ready. A cup of water and a piece of fruit are helpful in the first lessons. Have them handy before taking the bird out of its cage. You may also find a couple of whole peanuts helpful, as well as a millet spray.

CLIPPING A WING

Clipping a wing is a helpful aid to taming a wild bird. Do not clip a bird that will be left in an outdoor aviary. There is no reason to clip your bird's wing unless you truly intend to tame it. If you are unfamiliar with the procedure, do not attempt the clipping yourself. No book in the world can give you the necessary experience. Read the description to acquaint yourself with wing clipping, then find someone experienced who will follow the procedure recommended on these pages. (Perhaps your pet shop will do the clipping before you take your new bird home.)

To clip the wing, you will need good lighting, sharp scissors, a styptic powder (ask your pet shop) and a small pair of unused (sharp) wire cutters (get them at the hardware store). Styptic pencils are too hard and will not work well on feathers.

Two people should work together: one to hold the bird and watch it for any signs of stress, the other to do the actual clipping.

Most often you will only have to clip the primary and secondary flight feathers on one wing to achieve the desired result. Occasionally, you may have to take a few feathers off the other wing if the bird is an unusually strong flyer.

Some people recommend plucking the feathers instead of clipping; plucked feathers grow back faster, but I do not like feather plucking for the following reasons. Feather replacement is normally done gradually. It is a strain on the bird's system to have to regrow too many feathers at one time. Wild birds will be under enough stress in the taming

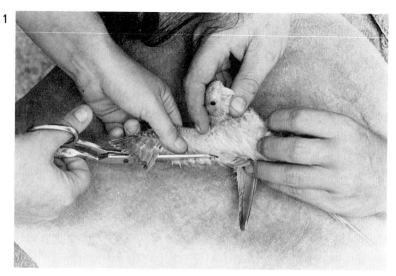

1. Two people should work together when clipping the wing or the claws. One person holds the bird securely while the other performs the clipping. Use sharp scissors to cut the flight feathers on the inside of one wing. Be very careful not to cut the feathers too close to the wing; if you do, the bird may have difficulty replacing these feathers later. 2. A pair of small wire cutters is a good tool for cutting the tips of the claws. Cut off only an eighth of an inch at a time. If you cut too much, the claw will bleed.

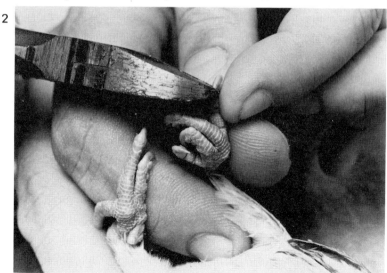

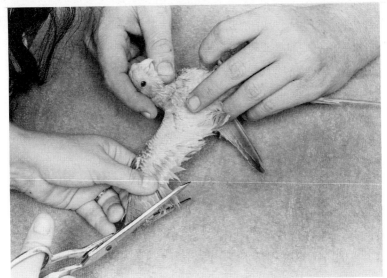

3. Outer primary flight feathers should be cut on *one wing only*. Use scissors to cut straight across the first four or five feathers, leaving half of their total length to protect the edge of the wing. 4. Note the comparison of the clipped wing and the unclipped wing. When clipping is properly done, only one wing need be cut to prevent flight.

routine without the additional stress of feather replacement. A second reason is this: all new feathers begin as blood feathers. Blood feathers have soft sheaths and are filled with blood to nourish the new feather as it grows. If feathers are plucked, blood feathers will appear in a relatively short time, perhaps before the rigors of taming are over. Any time the bird bumps the wing, there is a risk of breaking a blood feather. If broken or cracked, the blood feather will bleed until either the blood clots or the feather is pulled. It is easy to see why clipping the feathers is a better option than plucking.

The amount of time between clippings will vary slightly with different individuals. Some birds grow feathers more quickly than other birds. A good clipping should last for at least four months, possibly longer. Check the feather growth periodically. After a year or so, you will be able to estimate how often the wing will need to be clipped.

CAPTURING AND HOLDING THE BIRD

Use a towel or net to capture the bird. Throw either device over the bird's head to cover the beak. With one hand, grab the bird around the head and neck, from behind. Have the other person untangle the feet from the net or towel. While the other holds the feet, slip your free hand under the net to get the head out. Sometimes it is easier to leave the bird's head in the net or towel and hold the feet below the material. If this does not hamper the person doing the clipping, fine.

If you can, it is better to get the bird's head free to help you keep track of its respiration and pupillary responses. These are the two factors that will help you determine when the bird is experiencing too much stress.

Keep a finger of one hand between the bird's legs. With the other hand, grasp the head firmly but gently, cradling the neck with your third, fourth and fifth fingers. Be careful not to pull or push on the neck. Use a padded counter top or your lap covered with a towel to give yourself a safe holding platform. Keep your thumb under the lower mandible to control the head and keep it from twisting. Do not press on the bird's breast or abdomen.

The holder is responsible for making sure that the bird is not subjected to too much stress during wing or claw clipping. The method for holding the bird is the same for both procedures.

If the pupils of the eyes stop reacting to light or if the respiration becomes unusually rapid, the bird is under great stress. In this case you should carefully return the bird to its cage. Leave it alone and quiet; give it ample recovery time. Continue the clipping another day, not immediately after the bird regains its composure.

To avoid stressing the bird, gather all of the necessary equipment and plan beforehand exactly what you intend to do. During the procedure work quickly but carefully.

HOW TO CLIP THE WING

Extend both wings and look for blood feathers and broken feathers. If one wing is in great shape and the other has some broken feathers, clip the one with the breakage.

Hold the wing at the bend, not at the tip. Push back the small under-covert feathers and look at the shafts of the feathers as they come out of the wing. If there are blood feathers present you must be careful not to cut them. You should also leave the feathers on either side of a blood feather somewhat longer to give it additional protection. If you cut away the feathers on either side, the blood feather is more likely to break during taming.

Blood feathers are not difficult to identify. They have soft sheaths filled with blood and will appear bluish in color. If you compare these bluish sheaths with the beige-colored shafts of a fully grown feather, the difference becomes obvious. The sheaths of blood feathers are also thicker than the shafts of fully grown feathers. If you have any doubts at all about identifying blood feathers, do not attempt to clip the bird. You do not have enough experience.

Clip the first four flight feathers (counting from the tip of the wing), leaving half or three quarters of the feather in the wing.

Beginning with the fifth feather, clip at least eight more feathers. Leave at least ¾ inch of feather shaft sticking out of the wing. Be certain not to clip these feathers any closer to the wing, or it may cause the bird trouble later on. In all you may clip twelve to fourteen feathers. This is plenty and will surely keep the bird from flying.

Do not clip both wings using this method, for in so doing you will take away any chance the bird has of protecting its body and wing bones from injury if it falls. If you must clip a few feathers on the second wing (very unlikely), *do not* clip the first four feathers. Skip the first four and clip the fourth through the seventh or eighth feathers. Again check to be sure not to clip the feathers too close to the wing. Before clipping the second wing, give the bird a chance to try to fly. It probably won't be able to, making clipping both wings unnecessary.

RELEASING THE BIRD

After clipping is completed you have two options. The first is to place the bird back into its cage. The other is to begin taming it. If you decide to begin taming, go to the prepared taming area and place the bird down on the floor. Release the feet first. Then release the head. Step back and give the bird a minute to discover that it can no longer fly. It will surely try.

Never place a newly wing-clipped ringnecked parakeet on a bird stand. It will immediately attempt to fly and will probably take a fall.

CLIPPING THE CLAWS

As with the wing, you must be experienced before attempting to clip the claws. Every claw has a blood vessel running into it. You should be able to estimate the distance from the tip of the claw to the end of the vessel. If you clip the vessel it will undoubtedly bleed. The amount of bleeding depends upon how rapidly the bird's heart is beating and how much coagulant is in the blood. New birds often have vitamin deficiencies that may keep the blood from clotting normally.

Gather the equipment that you will use during the pedicure. Work in good light and use the same small wire cutters to clip the claws that you used to clip the wing. Have a nail file handy to smooth off the rough edges after you clip each claw. It is imperative that you have a good styptic powder handy before beginning to clip the claws. If you do hit blood, you won't waste a lot of time looking for the powder. Peroxide won't clot the blood sufficiently.

Clip no more than ¼ inch off the claw at first. You should not hit any vessel if you adhere to this maximum clipping distance. You can take off more of the claw later if you want to, but you cannot put it back. Clip all eight claws. Then file each one. Sometimes you may hit blood when filing the claws. If so, don't file that particular claw further; go on to the next one.

When a claw starts to bleed, take the styptic powder and press a small amount of the *dry* powder onto the bleeding tip. Hold it there for a few seconds. If the bleeding has stopped when you remove the pressure, go on and finish the pedicure. If the claw bleeds copiously, take a piece of dry cotton and put a good amount of styptic powder on it. Press the powder in the cotton against the bleeding tip and hold it there for at least thirty seconds. The bleeding should stop by then. If not, hold longer, using pressure if necessary.

Once the bleeding has subsided you can go on to finish the clipping. If the bleeding was severe, it is better to skip the rest of the clipping and put the bird back in its cage. Let it rest. Don't keep bothering it, or the blood won't have a chance to clot.

On newly acquired birds the vessel is often closer to the tip of the claw because the nails have probably never been clipped. With repeated clipping, the vessel will recede in the nail. Be very careful clipping the claws of new birds.

In case of badly overgrown claws, do not attempt the first pedicure without taking the bird to the vet. The blood vessel in overgrown claws is also overgrown. It is fairly likely that you will get some bleeding when clipping badly overgrown claws. Occasionally, styptic powder is not effective enough to stop bleeding quickly. The vet has medicines that clot the blood quickly and effectively.

You may find it necessary to clip the claws often, every two months or so. If you keep the bird on natural wood perches, you can probably increase this interval to four months or more. Natural wood helps wear down the claws gradually. Birds kept outdoors should never need their claws clipped.

TRIMMING THE BEAK

You should never have to clip the beak of your ring-necked parakeet if you provide the cuttlebone and mineral block suggested in the discussion on feeding. You may also provide additional chewing material like wood scraps to keep the beak trim.

Do not trim the beak yourself. Go to the vet and have him do it. This is best, because you may hit a blood vessel in the beak. It is sometimes difficult to stop bleeding from the beak, but the vet will have the means to do it.

THE FIRST TAMING LESSONS

After a one-week acclimation period, you are ready to begin the serious matter of taming your ringnecked parakeet. Go to the prepared taming area and take the bird cage with you. Place it on the floor near the bird stand and open the door.

Avoid commotion. Work quietly; move slowly and deliberately. Fast, abrupt movements will frighten the bird. You should have your two training sticks with you.

Many birds refuse to come out of the cage at first. See if the ringneck will perch on the short stick while still in the cage. It is often futile to try to draw it through the cage door, even if the bird will stand on the stick. Instead, just try to acquaint the bird with the stick and with you. Talk softly to the bird and tell it its name.

Some bird cages have a top that is removable. With other cages try taking out the bottom if the bird has not ventured near the door. You can try leaving the room for a moment to see if the bird will come out when you are not there. If so, fine. Close the door behind the bird, pick up your training stick and begin. One other way of getting the bird out of the cage is to stand behind the cage, leave the door open and slowly move your hands around the top and sides of the cage. Some birds will hop out the open door when you do this. Be patient when trying to get the bird out of the cage. It is best not to grab the bird to get it out.

BEGINNING STICK TRAINING

Ringnecks are high-strung birds and may need a few lessons to learn to perch on the training stick. Work low, near the floor. Put the stick in front of the bird and press lightly against its chest with the stick. Most birds will jump away from the stick at first. Be patient.

Keep placing the stick in front of the ringneck until it lifts a foot and steps onto the stick. It may place only one foot on the stick. If it stays still with one foot on the stick and one foot on the floor, remain where you are for at least a few seconds. Then slowly roll the stick to make the bird place its foot back down on the floor.

Repeat the steps of placing the stick in front of the bird, getting it to step on it, remaining still and then stepping back to the floor. Try to get the bird to place both feet on

1. Retrieve the ringneck with a training stick if it jumps to the floor or windowsill. 2. Use the stick to carry the bird from its cage to the bird stand.

3. If the bird does not step easily from stick to stand, try turning the stick diagonally. Remember that individual birds differ from one to another in their temperaments and that different birds sometimes require slightly different approaches. It is all right to vary your technique slightly from bird to bird as long as the basic principles underlying the training process are observed. 4. Most birds will climb from the lower point of the stick to the higher stand.

4

the stick as soon as possible. Be very still when your ringneck does this the first time. Have the bird sit on the stick, then roll the stick to make it step down.

Do not lift the stick high above the floor until the bird willingly steps onto the stick and remains there without jumping away. When you do finally lift the stick off the floor, do it very slowly. Be very quiet and still when you get it two to three feet off the floor. Stand still with the bird. Place it back down on the floor after a few minutes.

The object of stick training is to teach the bird to step up onto a perch and down off without hesitation. You use the stick to teach this behavior without exposing yourself to unnecessary bites. Once the bird has, in your estimation, mastered the skills of stick training, you can move on to the next step: the bird stand.

TRAINING THE BIRD TO THE STAND

With the bird sitting quietly on the training stick, move slowly to the bird stand. Place the bird and stick behind the stand, and then roll the stick slightly to encourage the ringneck to step from the stick to the crossbar of the stand. Your bird may do this right away, or it may jump to the floor and run away.

If you have a bird that jumps, just retrieve it with the training stick and once again move to the stand. Keep repeating this procedure until the ringneck steps onto the stand. Remain standing in front of the bird to help steady it on the stand. After a couple of minutes, try to have the bird step back onto the stick. Let it remain there; then place it back onto the bird stand.

Drill the bird in stepping from the stick to the bird stand and back again. This drill is a very important preliminary step to hand training. Make certain that the bird performs these behaviors well; then move on to hand training.

HAND TRAINING

Diligent training to the stick and bird stand will pay off when you begin hand taming. Birds that have learned to step up onto perches and off again are less likely to bite your hand. You must remember to move slowly when hand-training your ringneck. It may seem that the bird is regressing, jumping away from you to the floor. This is to be expected in the initial hand-taming lessons.

Use your training stick to retrieve the bird from the floor if it jumps. Return it to the stand. Place your hand in front of the bird. Speak to the bird softly to distract it. Move your free hand slowly in front of the bird and to the right or left of the hand that you want it to step on. Never threaten your ringneck with your free hand; just use it for the purpose of distracting the bird.

As in stick training, your bird may place one foot onto your hand while keeping the other on the bird stand. That's fine for starters. Coax the bird to step on with both feet. Talk to it. Remain very still in front of the bird. Rest your hand on the crossbar of the stand. This will give you stability, and thus the bird will feel more comfortable on your hand.

Do not move away from the stand with the bird on your hand. Walking with the bird comes later. Now it is important only to teach the bird to step onto your hand from the stand. For a few lessons just work on this skill. You can't rush the bird, so be happy when you have the bird sitting on your hand, even if you do have to stay at the stand.

Placing the bird onto the stand and coaxing it back up to your hand is your main concern in hand taming. Use your own judgment as to when to begin walking with the bird. Remain in the taming area to start. Turn your back to the bird stand with the bird on your hand. Then turn back again and place it on the stand.

1

Ringnecks love raw corn on the cob (1), millet spray (2) and peanuts (3). Any of these foods can be used as a training reward or a treat.

3 →

2

BITING

It is likely that you will get bitten once or twice while taming a wild ringnecked parakeet. *Never* strike the bird for biting; it won't do any good. Birds like the ringneck do not understand what to you is a natural reaction. Remember how small the ringneck is; you could easily injure it if you hit it. Birds bite from fear more than from aggression. Just stay calm, remove the bird's beak from your finger and start again.

Once the bird learns to trust you, biting behavior will diminish and then disappear. Try pushing a piece of millet spray or apple into the bird's mouth if it persists in biting. Go back to stick training, if necessary, until the bird becomes more familiar with you. To counter biting, always offer it a treat and a kind word at the end of each lesson. Feeding the bird from your hand is one of the best ways to make friends with it. Do not get discouraged. Hand-taming the bird may take twenty to thirty lessons.

LENGTH AND FREQUENCY
OF TAMING LESSONS

Two or three half-hour lessons a day are about all that a working person can devote to taming a bird. Whenever possible, give the lesson several times a day for twenty to thirty minutes. Between lessons you can place the bird back into its cage, but if you are going to be around, leave it sitting on the stand. This will help train the bird to remain sitting on the stand for extended periods of time.

Most ringnecked parakeets are very comfortable on a bird stand. Once familiar with it they will sit for hours at a time. Of course, your bird will jump from time to time if something startles it. Just retrieve it with your hand or stick and place it back on the stand. You can help the bird become happy on the stand by attaching a millet spray or chewy toy to the crossbar. You will be surprised to find your bird playing, eating and sleeping on the stand.

Never chain your ringneck to the bird stand. This is unnecessary and inadvisable. The bird could twist its leg severely if chained. If you follow the recommendations for training the bird to the stand you will never be tempted to chain the bird.

SPEECH TRAINING

You can begin speech training immediately after getting the ringneck. Some prove to be good talkers, although their voices are very high-pitched. They can learn to copy whistles and tunes in addition to words and short phrases.

Talk to your bird in a clear tone of voice, repeating just one word at first. Be sure to speak slowly and to *over-* enunciate each syllable of the word. Start with "hello," followed by the bird's name. Keep working on that one word until the bird responds appropriately.

Be realistic when deciding what to teach the bird to say. A woman often makes a better speech trainer because her voice is usually higher pitched than a man's. The most important qualities of a successful speech trainer are the determination to stick with the training, over-enunciation of each syllable to be taught and clarity of the voice.

The best times of day for speech training are in the morning and late afternoon. Listen to your ringneck, and you will soon discover when he is naturally vocal. You don't have to give formal lessons, with the room dark and the cage covered. I have never found dark rooms or cage covers to be of any help in speech training. Just talk to your bird for five or ten minutes several times during the day—especially in the morning and afternoon.

If you hear the bird attempting to say something and you recognize it as something you were teaching, immediately say the word or phrase to your bird. Listen for it to repeat what you have said. Very often the bird's first attempts at speech will occur in this way. These are very exciting,

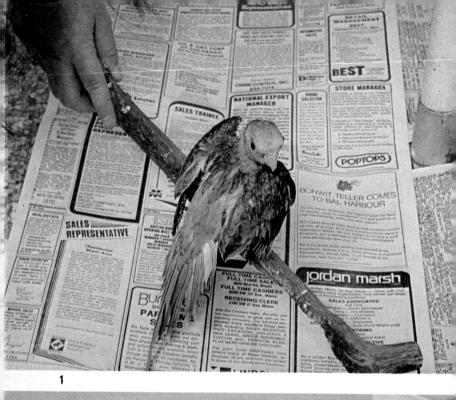

1

1. During the first lessons, teach your ringneck to step onto a training stick. Work low to the floor and expect your new bird to jump around for a while. 2. When you want the bird to turn around, try touching the tail lightly. 3. When your new bird steps onto the bird stand for the first time, step back and let it relax for a while.

← 2

special moments, and you will surely be encouraged to continue speech training.

It may take several weeks, even months, before your ringneck says its first word. If you work seriously at training the bird to talk, very likely it will get around to talking.

You may want to invest in recorded speech lessons for your ringnecked parakeet. I don't use them, but you may find them helpful if you must work all day. Very few people want to talk to their bird after a hard day's work. The recorded lessons may break the ice for you. Once the bird begins talking, take over the lessons in person.

SUMMARY

Choose your ringneck carefully, using the criterion of good health. Feed and house it properly. Approach taming with self-confidence and determination. Consult a vet whenever you suspect illness; don't delay. Above all, remember that you will get what you pay for. The bargain bird is rarely a real bargain.

A bell and dog choke collar attached to the bird stand make a good toy for your pet ringneck. Your bird may spend hours climbing up and down on the chain.

Food rewards help establish a good rapport between you and the ringneck. The bird may throw the proffered treats away at first but will soon learn to enjoy food rewards.

Left: Ringnecks fly to the highest point of the cage and hang from the sides when disturbed by intruders. *Below:* A spacious outdoor aviary can house a large colony of ringnecks, but breeding pairs may produce more young when housed one pair to a flight cage.

Breeding Ringnecked Parakeets

Successful breeding of ringnecked parakeets depends upon obtaining birds of the opposite sex (females are hard to come by), pairing compatible birds of breeding age, providing the proper environment and feeding an enriched diet. The birds should be in perfect condition and be eating well before you set them up for breeding.

The breeding cage must be large enough for the birds to fly in. Four feet square and 4½ to 5 feet high is a good size for one pair. Although you can breed several pairs in a colony, I have had much more success with a single pair in a cage. A separate pair do not have to contend with the interference of other ringnecks in the aviary and usually are

1

1. A towel can be used to capture and hold a bird for clipping or administering medication—or just for holding the bird so that it can be examined. The use of a towel is preferable to the use of gloves during these procedures. 2. Place the towel over the bird. Wrap it around the bird's body and (3) be sure to leave the head free so that the bird can breathe.

3 →

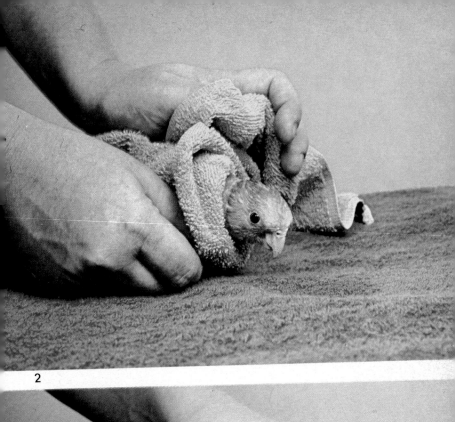

2

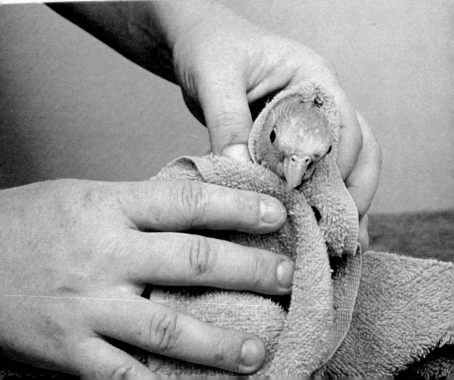

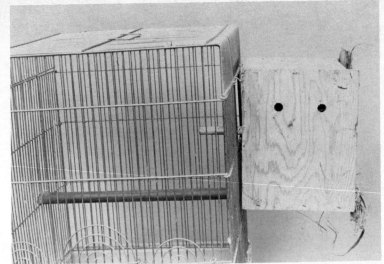

1. Fresh green leafy vegetables are an important part of the bird's daily diet and are needed to produce healthy birds such as (2) this mature pair of Plum-headed Parakeets. 3. This nest box is for use with lovebirds and is too small for ringnecks. 4. A good ringneck nest box would be fourteen inches long, twelve inches deep and twelve inches high.

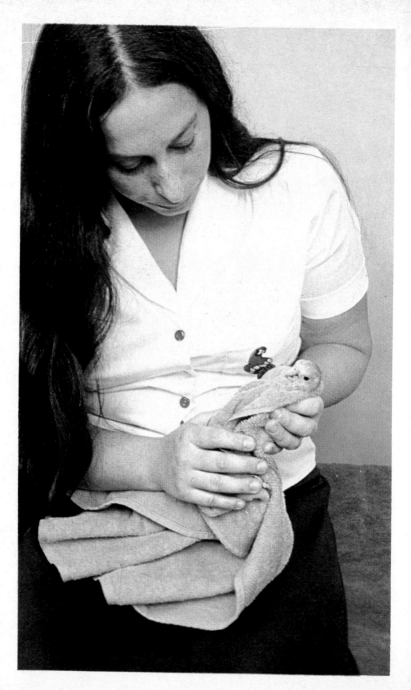

2

1. Hold the bird in a towel to examine it for injury. 2. If you must touch the face or eyes, use a sterile cotton swab, not your fingers. Hold the head gently but firmly when working around the bird's eyes. Be careful not to cover the nostrils.

← 1

able to hatch and rear greater numbers of young. In addition, ringnecked parakeets are unusually aggressive when the urge to nest is upon them. It is not unusual to find that a pair will be chased out of their nest box by one of their neighbors, who will then break the eggs or kill any babies that may have hatched. The sitting female ringneck can be injured severely by the intruder, for she will fight to protect her chicks.

The breeding box must be at least 14 inches long, 10 to 12 inches deep and 10 to 12 inches high. The entrance hole, about 3 inches in diameter, should be close to the top of the box and over to one side (rather than in the middle). There should be a short perch outside of the entrance hole to facilitate entering and leaving the box. Fill the bottom of the nest box with pine or cedar chips (shavings work well also) to a depth of 4 to 6 inches. Ringnecked parakeets like to dig out a nest hollow in the wood chips. Evidence of their entering the box is definite when you find wood chips scattered below the nest entrance.

THE BREEDING SEASON

The time your birds will breed depends on the climate. I have had the best yields of chicks in the spring and early summer. The beginning of the rainy season seems to stimulate the birds to begin nesting, though motivated pairs will begin breeding in any weather and in any season. Most ringnecks will establish their own regular breeding cycle and stick to it.

DIET

For reproduction the regular maintenance diet that has already been discussed will have to be enriched. Increase the amount of fruits and vegetables that you feed the birds. Raw corn and apple are eaten in copious amounts by my Plum-heads when they are nesting. Give at least four different fruits and vegetables every day. Offer larger amounts of green leafy vegetables. Increase the dosage of vitamins and make certain the gravel mixture is fresh. Mineral block is important during egg formation. You may add an oil supplement to the diet; use cod-liver or wheat-germ oil sparingly on the seed.

THE EGGS AND INCUBATION

Ringnecked parakeets usually lay between four and seven eggs. Yours may lay fewer or more. The birds may not hatch all of the eggs, or if they do, they may let the smallest chick die if they decide they can't raise it too.

The female sits on the eggs throughout incubation, which lasts from twenty-one to twenty-five days. The climate and humidity in the nest box will affect the incubation time. In my aviary female Plum-heads seem to go into a trance when they begin incubating the eggs. The wildest, biting hens become docile and touchable when sitting. This does not mean you should bother the hen when she is sitting, as too much interference from you may cause her to desert the nest.

The male visits the female often, bringing her food and keeping her company during the day. At night the male remains outside of the nest, keeping guard against predators.

The female will occasionally leave the nest to get a drink of water or eat a bit, but the male is very conscientious about bringing her whole pieces of fruit and sections of millet spray that she can eat while she sits on the eggs. The oval eggs are white in color and slightly larger than Cockatiel eggs. They are oval-shaped.

THE HATCHLINGS

The babies will begin peeping inside of the shell and can be heard before they hatch. They break out early in the morning and have a bit of yellow fluff when they emerge wet from the egg. The down soon dries, and it is gone by the fourth day after hatching. The chicks remain naked until

1

3

1 and 2. Do not hold the wing too far out by the tips of the flight feathers. Grip the wing close to the wing bend to prevent injury.

3. Your bird may enjoy chewing up hibiscus flowers or other fresh branches with leaves. Be absolutely certain that the flowers or branches are completely insecticide-free before letting your bird chew them.

← 2

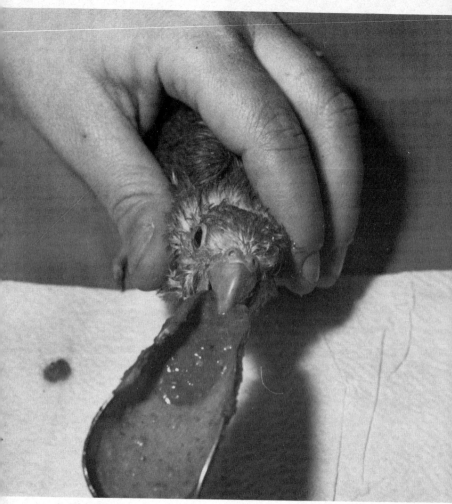

1. This Plum-head parakeet chick is about 4½ weeks old. Learning to eat formula from a spoon can be messy for both the bird and its foster parent.

2

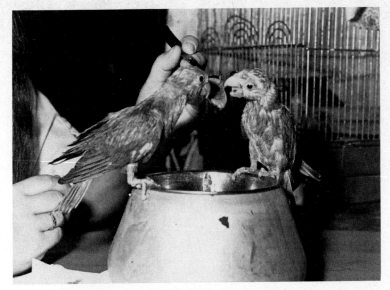

2. Two chicks sit atop the formula dish and eat from the same spoon. They are highly competitive even at this early age. 3. Some chicks have to be given special attention to make sure that they get enough at each feeding. Hand-raising baby birds is time-consuming and can be a frustrating chore. Whenever possible, it is best to let the parent birds rear their own young.

3

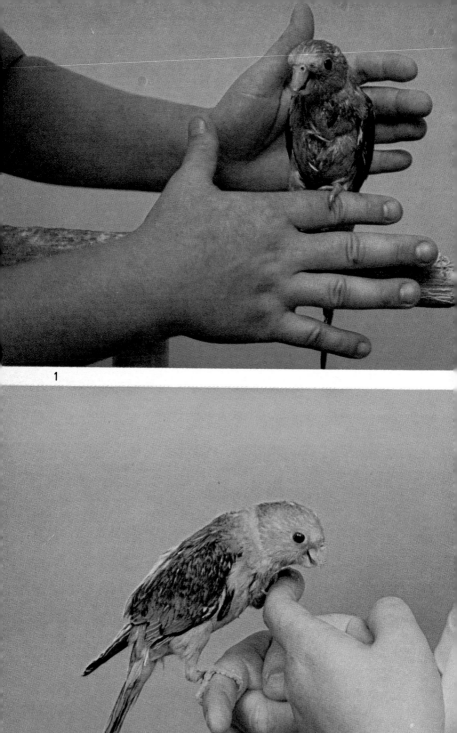

1

1. Training the ringneck to step from the bird stand to your hand requires time, patience and a determined trainer. 2. Offer a finger on alternating hands once the bird learns to step up without fear. 3. When the ringneck accepts your finger or hand as a secure perch, congratulate yourself for a job well done!

3

←2

their pin feathers appear in approximately two and a half to three weeks.

Both the mother and father feed the chicks. The big feedings given four times a day are supplemented in between by smaller feedings. The parents eat large amounts of seeds, greens, fruits and vegetables, which they then regurgitate in a partially digested form into the babies' mouths.

As the babies grow older and larger, their cries for food become stronger and more demanding. The parents must constantly visit the food dishes and the chicks throughout the day into the early evening. I have not observed the parents feeding chicks during the night.

At four weeks of age the babies are covered with feathers, although the tail feathers are very short. Their beaks have started changing color from black to whatever is normal for their species. They remain inside the nest box for the first six weeks of life.

When the babies begin venturing out of the nest box they will crowd around the nest entrance and peer out. The boldest chick (not always the oldest) tries to push the others out of the way to get the best view. Already they begin competing with one another for dominance. The chicks run back to the nest box for protection when humans or animals approach unexpectedly.

By seven weeks of age most ringnecked chicks are out of the nest box for good. The parents continue to feed them for another week or so, but the babies soon learn to eat on their own. Initially they eat mostly fruits and greens, along with large amounts of millet spray. Cracking sunflower seeds and peanuts comes later.

ABUSED OR ABANDONED CHICKS

Most ringnecked parakeets are good parents. Occasionally you may encounter pairs or individual birds (usually the male) that desert their young. In most cases the female is not responsible for deserting the young. Since she does have to depend greatly on the male for rearing the young successfully, if he is unable or unwilling to assist her in rearing the young, there is little that she can do except desert the nestlings.

In some cases you may find that your male is not just neglecting the chicks but is actually abusing them. I had one male that would take each chick within one hour of its hatching and throw it out of the nest. He did this with six babies, all of which survived when hand-fed.

Other males will peck the babies, eventually killing them. Again there is very little that the female can do to prevent her mate from killing the babies. She is often in the state of passivity described earlier. The reason that ringnecks refuse to care for their chicks after incubating the eggs is very puzzling. I have not had enough opportunity to observe this behavior in ringnecked parakeets, but perhaps a pattern of behavior will develop as I record more observations of breeding pairs.

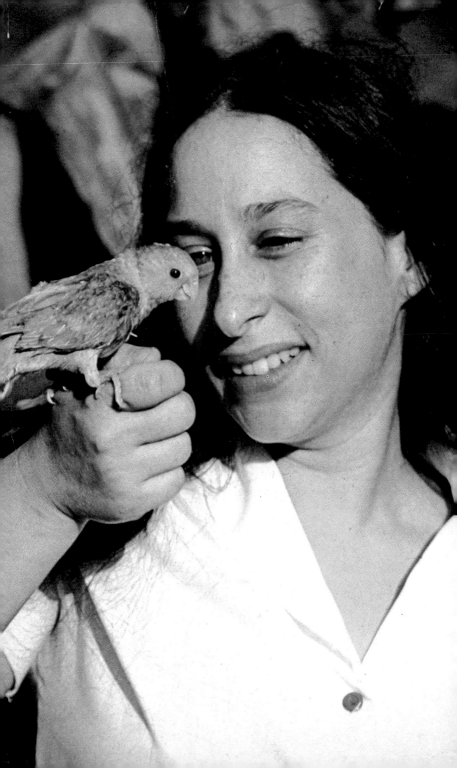